Men are anxious to improve their circumstances,
but are unwilling to improve themselves;
they therefore remain bound.

James Allen

MY LIFE

Author **Lyzz Yamazaki**
Illustration **Ayumi Ishikawa**
Binding and design **Shimpachi Inoue**

Translated by **Raju R. Thakrar**
Arranged by **TranNet KK**

Printed in Canada

Published by **One Peace Books, Inc., New York, New York**

One Peace Books, Inc.
57 GREAT JONES STREET NEW YORK, NY 10012 USA
TEL: 212-260-4400 FAX: 212-995-2969
URL : http://www.onepeacebooks.com

ISBN 978-0978508494

my life

Written *Lyzz Yamazaki*
Illustrated *Ayumi Ishikawa*

For starters

When a person goes to a hospital and the doctor asks what their problem is, is there anybody out there who would say they don't know? If so, they're probably crazy.

In a restaurant, you won't be served anything unless you place an order. Have you ever heard of a person who, without ordering something, screams, "What an inconsiderate restaurant!" and gets angry and cries? If there is such a person, they're probably dangerous!

Nevertheless, my experience in psychotherapy has shown me that there are a surprisingly high number of people like this out there. In other words, there are an unexpectedly high number of people who just complain without knowing themselves or their lifestyle, or who are at a loss and get down or irritated, without thinking about ways to improve things.

I think that what lies behind worries like these is the fundamental problem of not knowing yourself. You need to believe in yourself in order to bring out your potential. In order to believe in yourself, you need to know your true self.

"To know" here also means "notice." What do you like? What do you hate? What kinds of things hurt you? What kinds of things make you feel joy? What kind of life do you want to lead in the future?

You need to discover what's best for you, not just what people have always told you is good. If you realize who you really are, and then base your thinking on this aspect of yourself, you can definitely be confident of your own individual values and the life path you want to follow. In this respect, it's very, very important to know yourself.

This book is here for you to learn about yourself. Please answer the questions that follow. I think that by answering the questions you'll come to understand that your reality is not simply coincidental, but that you are creating it. What's more, by improving the habits from which you weave your reality, you will solve your current problems and achieve your goals.

Any kind of book that claims to help you become the person you want to be is appealing. It may be energizing to be told that you're lucky, but if you don't know yourself, there's not much you can do with just that information.

You have freedom and value, as well as the right to become happy. In order to claim that, you need to know yourself. If you want to encounter your true self and fulfill your dreams, I invite you to have fun making this book your very own.

CONTENTS

Before answering the questions

As you answer the questions, I'd like you to bear in mind the following four things:

There are no questions that you "must" answer. Answer freely and honestly.

Don't think of any of the questions as strange; instead, answer frankly and in a relaxed manner. You don't need to overdo your answers, or answer as if you're being watched by someone. Even if such an "unnatural you" tries to change things, there's no guarantee that it will make you happy. So please just listen to what your heart is saying. Feel free to draw a picture if you like. Please just try to enjoy the feeling of liberation that this book provides.

Answer the questions unconditionally.

There will probably be some questions that when answering you find yourself hesitating with thoughts like "however..." or "but I could say...". Pay no attention to such thoughts.

The same applies to questions where you may initially think "Can I, or can't I?" Put aside any worries about whether you can answer, and just answer. This approach will help your potential grow rapidly.

It's OK if you take your time. Complete the book.

This book will be complete when you've answered all the questions.

If you think a question is hard to answer, it's OK to leave it and go on to the next one. Don't worry if it takes you six months or a year — please just finish the book. When you see a question for which you don't know the answer, mull it over. If you're a person who immediately thinks "I don't know," you most likely have a tendency to leave many things in an "I don't know" state. Instead, consider that in searching for an answer you are cultivating your mind.

Be aware that you are facing your true self.

I think that the process of answering these questions will bring about various realizations; and realities and feelings that you have to face will come to the surface. When this happens, it's perfectly natural for you to feel discomfort, or even strong discontent with yourself. That's proof that your true self is being brought out—so these are, in fact, feelings that you should welcome. Instead of running away from these feelings, please try to enjoy them as much as you possibly can.

Answer all the questions with love.

CHAPTER **1**

Introduction

As a warm-up exercise, list some basic information about yourself and your environment. Answer freely and honestly.

Gender:

_____

Star sign:

_____

Birthplace:

_____

The person who named you:

_____

The hopes that your name contains:

_____

_____

_____

Nickname:

_____

_____

_____

Catchphrase you might use in describing yourself:

_____

_____

_____

_____

_____

Animal you would compare yourself to:

_____

_____

_____

_____

_____

Three words or expressions you like:

_____

_____

_____

_____

Your motto in life:

Interests and hobbies:

Words and phrases that you often use:

_____

_____

_____

_____

_____

_____

_____

_____

_____

Customs and habits you want to change:

_____

_____

_____

_____

_____

_____

_____

Things you collect:

Earliest childhood memory:

Most serious illness you've had:

Things you want to throw away but can't:

_____

_____

_____

_____

_____

_____

_____

_____

_____

_____

_____

_____

_____

_____

_____

_____

Kindergarten and nursery school you went to:

Elementary school you went to:

Junior high school you went to:

High school you went to:

University or vocational school you went to:

Favorite season:

_____

_____

Favorite color:

_____

_____

Favorite number:

_____

_____

Favorite food:

_____

_____

Favorite fruit:

_____

_____

Favorite flower:

_____

_____

Favorite smell or fragrance:

_____

_____

Favorite animal:

_____

_____

Favorite drink:

_____

_____

Pet you have or would like to have:

_____

_____

Sport you most like watching:

_____

_____

Sport you most like doing:

_____

_____

Favorite hangout:

_____

_____

Favorite theme park:

_____

_____

Places you want to go overseas:

_____

_____

_____

_____

_____

_____

_____

_____

_____

_____

_____

Places you want to go in your own country:

Sights you want to see once before you die:

----

chapter 1

Places you want to travel to by yourself:

_____

_____

_____

_____

_____

_____

_____

_____

Places that make you feel tired:

_____

_____

_____

_____

_____

_____

_____

_____

Songs that perk you up:

_____

_____

_____

_____

_____

_____

_____

_____

Songs you feel like hearing when you have a broken heart:

_____

_____

_____

_____

_____

_____

_____

_____

Songs you feel like hearing before going to sleep:

Songs you feel like hearing while driving:

Favorite musician:

_____

_____

_____

_____

_____

_____

_____

_____

Movies that perk you up:

_____

_____

_____

_____

_____

_____

_____

_____

Movies you feel like seeing when you have a broken heart:

_____

_____

_____

_____

_____

_____

_____

_____

Movies you've seen many times:

_____

_____

_____

_____

_____

_____

_____

_____

Favorite actress:

Favorite actor:

TV programs that you watch without fail:

Favorite romantic novel:

- -

- -

- -

Favorite mystery novel:

- -

- -

- -

Favorite essay:

- -

- -

- -

Favorite writer:

- -

- -

- -

Write down how you spend a weekday, from when you wake up to when you go to sleep:

Write down how you spend a day off, from when you wake up to when you go to sleep:

_____

_____

_____

_____

_____

_____

_____

_____

_____

_____

_____

_____

_____

_____

_____

First thing you do after waking up:

- -

- -

- -

- -

- -

First thing you do after coming home:

- -

- -

- -

- -

- -

- -

Place where you spend the most time at home:

- -

- -

- -

- -

- -

Average number of hours of sleep:

_____

☐ Want to sleep more? ☐ Just right? ☐ Want to sleep less?

Things in your room or at work that relax you:

_____

_____

_____

_____

_____

_____

If you don't have such a thing, what kind of thing would relax you?

_____

_____

_____

_____

_____

_____

● "Time" or "action" you want to increase in the space of a day:

✱ Reasons:

✱ Effects that increasing it/them would have:

● "Time" or "action" you want to decrease in the space of a day:

✱ Reasons:

✱ Effects that decreasing it/them would have:

Aspects of the house or apartment you live in that you like:

_____

_____

_____

_____

_____

_____

_____

_____

_____

_____

_____

_____

_____

_____

_____

Aspects of the house or apartment you live in that you don't like:

_____

_____

_____

_____

_____

_____

_____

_____

_____

_____

_____

_____

_____

_____

_____

_____

Aspects of your neighborhood that you like:

Aspects of your neighborhood that are convenient:

_____

_____

_____

_____

_____

_____

_____

_____

_____

_____

_____

_____

_____

_____

_____

Aspects of your neighborhood that you don't like:

- -

- -

- -

- -

- -

- -

- -

- -

- -

- -

- -

- -

- -

- -

- -

Aspects of your neighborhood that are inconvenient:

_____

_____

_____

_____

_____

_____

_____

_____

_____

_____

_____

_____

_____

_____

_____

Area you would like to live in if you were to move:

_____

_____

_____

_____

_____

_____

_____

_____

_____

_____

_____

_____

_____

_____

_____

_____

chapter 1

Plan or layout of your room:

How would you rearrange it?

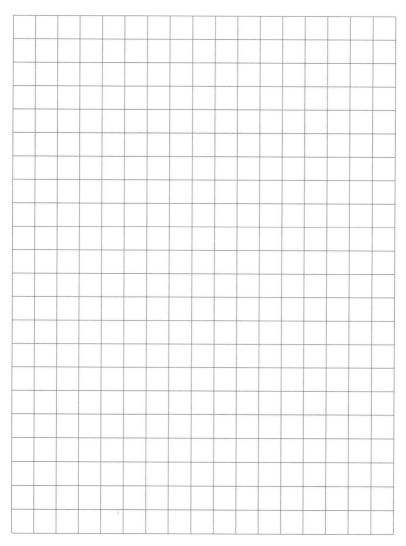

To those who have finished

CHAPTER

1

In Chapter 1, I had you answer some questions for basic information about yourself and your environment as a warm up exercise.

If you were able to answer freely and honestly while also having fun, then that's enough. And if you were able to realize something about your current lifestyle on top of that, then give yourself double brownie points!

You probably found many questions easy to answer. But maybe some questions required more time. This was likely due to one or both of the following main reasons:

(1) Simply because you'd never thought about such things before.
(2) Because thinking about them put you off.

If (1) applies to you, please don't be too concerned, because by thinking about and answering the rest of the questions in this book you will automatically be training yourself to come up with the answers. But if (2) applies to you then you should examine the reason why this is so. In other words, you should consider why you can't think and answer freely even though it's OK to do so. This exercise will help you to remove those personal limitations and restrictions that are invisible to you now.

There are no right or wrong answers. The main objective is to realize things about yourself and reality. Of course it would be even better if, from these answers, you were able to discover ways you could improve things. Ideally you will translate the things you've uncovered into action.

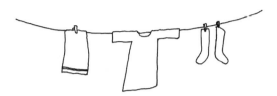

To achieve this you need to look at your answers from various angles. This means you need to realize:

• Where you are (your current condition; I call this "the starting point"].
• What your heart truly feels and desires.
• What the things are that can act as pointers for you to improve yourself, and what kind of things you can apply and put into practice from today onward.

Please work on your ability to notice things, so that you can receive as many messages as possible from the answers that you have given.

My self

In order to live as yourself, you need to accept yourself.

Take one more look at yourself.

● Are you currently happy?

☐ Yes   ☐ No

✷ Reasons:

Three of your strong points:

Three of your weak points:

Aspects of your face that you like:

Aspects of your face you might like to have plastic surgery on:

Things you say and do when you want to concentrate:

Things you say and do when you feel down:

Things you talk about first when you meet a friend you haven't seen in
a long time:

● Think of a time when you recently enjoyed yourself to your heart's content

* When and where?

* What happened?

● Think of a time when you recently had a good laugh.

✱ When and where?

_ _

_ _

_ _

_ _

_ _

✱ What happened?

_ _

_ _

_ _

_ _

_ _

● Think of a time when you recently felt outraged.

✳ When and where?

. _

. _

. _

. _

. _

✳ What happened?

. _

. _

. _

. _

. _

● Think of a time when you recently cried?

   ✱ When and where?

   ✱ What happened?

- Think of a time when you were recently hurt.

  * When and where?

  * What happened?

● Think of a time when you recently tried to gauge a person's feelings.

✱ When and where?

✱ What happened?

The gift that you were the most happy to receive in your life:

_____

_____

_____

_____

The words that have most hurt you in your life:

_____

_____

_____

_____

_____

The words that made you the happiest in your life:

_____

_____

_____

_____

_____

The thing you're proudest about in your life:

_____

_____

_____

_____

_____

The most embarrassing thing in your life:

_____

_____

_____

_____

The thing you most regret in your life:

_____

_____

_____

_____

_____

The luckiest thing that ever happened in your life:

_____

_____

_____

_____

_____

_____

_____

_____

If you were to congratulate yourself for working hard, what would you

have worked so hard on?

_____

_____

_____

_____

_____

_____

If you were to apologize to yourself, what would you apologize for?

_____

_____

_____

_____

_____

_____

If God told you that you are forgiven for your sins, what do you think

that forgiveness would be for?

_____

_____

_____

_____

_____

_____

_____

_____

List all the feelings that you are uncomfortable with and don't want to feel:

_____

_____

_____

_____

_____

_____

● When you suffer, do you eventually find peace of mind?

☐ Yes ☐ No

✱ Reasons:

_____

_____

_____

_____

✱ People who are connected with how you feel:

_____

_____

_____

_____

● In your heart, think of a child that you love.

✱ That child's appearance:

✱ That child's feelings:

● Now, think of a child that you really dislike.

✱ That child's appearance:

✱ That child's feelings:

● Now picture a child that you always make wait for what they want.

✱ That child's appearance:

_____

_____

_____

✱ That child's feelings:

_____

_____

If you were able to choose the time of your death, how old would you be?

_ Years old

People you would like to come back from the dead:

_ _

_ _

_ _

If you believe in reincarnation, what do you think you might have been
in that life?

_ _

_ _

_ _

If you were to be re-born, which gender would you be?

● ☐ Man   ☐ Woman

✱ Reasons:

_ _

_ _

_ _

Things that you used to play with as a child that you were crazy about:

_____

_____

_____

_____

_____

_____

● If you could return to your past, which time would you want to return to?

_____

_____

✶ Reasons:

_____

_____

_____

_____

_____

_____

_____

● List three things you would like to happen right now:

1. --

2. --

3. --

✱ Suppose each thing actually did happen. Think seriously about what would happen next. Then write down what you think would be the ultimate result, and your feelings, including how they might come about:

1. --

----

2. --

----

3. --

● List three things that, if they were to happen now, would put you in a difficult situation:

1. _____

2. _____

3. _____

✱ Suppose each thing actually did happen. Think seriously about what would happen next. Then write down what you think would be the ultimate result, and your feelings, including how they come about:

1. _____

_____

2. _____

_____

3. _____

_____

Try to list all the things you recall having acquired the ability to do,

from your birth until now:

● Supposing that the best health condition were 100 points, how many points would you currently have?

```
┌ ─ ─ ─ ─ ─ ─ ─ ─ ─ ─ ─ ┐
│                       │
│ _ _ _ _ _ _ _ points │
└ ─ ─ ─ ─ ─ ─ ─ ─ ─ ─ ─ ┘
```

✱ Reasons:

_____

_____

_____

✱ Things you are now doing to improve your health:

_____

_____

_____

_____

✱ Things you would like to do to improve your health:

_____

_____

_____

_____

Imagine that your body (legs, feet, brain, internal organs, etc.) works

for you like an employee and write it a letter of thanks:

_____

_____

_____

_____

_____

_____

_____

_____

_____

_____

_____

_____

_____

_____

_____

_____

Three things you would take to a desert island:

_____

_____

_____

Three things you would save from your house in the event of a fire:

_____

_____

_____

A story that you can brag about:

Moments when you hate yourself:

● A worry that you have now:

✳ Can it be resolved: ☐ Yes ☐ No

How would you resolve it?

........●.......●......●.....●.....●.........●.....●.......●.....●.......●.......●.....●.......●.....●.......●......●.....

● A worry that you have now:

✳ Can it be resolved: ☐ Yes ☐ No

How would you resolve it?

● A worry that you have now:

✱ Can it be resolved: ☐ Yes ☐ No

How would you resolve it?

........•.........•.......•.....•....•.......•...•...•.......•........•...•..•.......•.....•.......•......•.....•........•......

● A worry that you have now:

✱ Can it be resolved: ☐ Yes ☐ No

How would you resolve it?

List things that you definitely do not want to be in the future:

Image that a very happy child lives in your heart. What is that child

saying that he or she wants to do now?

What kinds of colors come to mind when you read each of the following words?

Love:

Fear:

Happiness:

Endurance:

Competition:

Jealousy:

Haste:

Loneliness:

Adventure:

Sincerity:

Anger:

Sadness:

Effort:

Freedom:

Justice:

● You want to live as your ideal self, but a person comes along who wants to throw you off-balance:

✳ Who would that person be?

_____

_____

_____

_____

✳ Face that person and state clearly and firmly how wonderful a thing it is to live as your ideal self:

_____

_____

_____

✳ If you were to wish or pray for something for yourself right now, what would that be?

_____

_____

_____

Complete the following sentences:

The real me is...

The real me wants to...

I want to always be a person who feels...

For you to have your "perfect environment" what things would be essential? There are no rules, so write as many things as you like, then number them in order of priority:

To those who finished

CHAPTER

2

In this chapter I had you answer questions about yourself. Did you have any sudden insights?

If there were any places where you were surprised at how you felt, then it can be said that your answers were meaningful enough. This is because, as we live within society, we lose sight of many things about ourselves. This means that we live under the illusion that our "provisional self" or "false self" is actually our "true self." Perhaps some of you were even shocked at noticing an unexpected aspect of yourselves... but please understand that this is an experience that you cannot avoid on the way to learning about your own "true self."

Here I'd like to make a few simple comments on your answers to the questions.

I created this book from the point of view that the most meaningful parts are those where you felt and realized things from the answers you wrote down about yourself. Thus I'll refrain from over-analyzing your answers. I'd like to help just enough that you can feel and realize even more.

Those who experienced an unpleasant feeling from any answer should not deny or push aside that feeling.

To learn about your true self is to accept yourself as you really are. Thus, it's important to accept even the self that is experiencing an unpleasant feeling. If, when you experience such a feeling, you find that you're feeling shaky, then tell yourself in your heart that this is natural and that you will be all right!

To those people who gave answers that were contradictory to what they think is good or how things should be: this is really amazing! This is because it shows that your values, based on the true you, came to the fore.

Since each of us wants to be a good person toward everybody, there is a tendency to end up lying to oneself. People become convinced that it's natural to choose what everybody else thinks is good. But please consider this: you are an individual, so there is no way that you can be a good person for everybody. The way you're supposed to be for everyone else is not necessarily the way you're supposed to be for yourself. How about immediately taking this opportunity to make choices and live a lifestyle that's based on the values of your true self that you discovered today?

You may have realized how much you value yourself and what kinds of things you are attached to or afraid of. If you felt love or hope, absorb them: imagine them spreading into your heart and settling there. Even if you experienced negative feelings, don't blame the person that you've been up to now. It would be a waste of time to reproach yourself for that, now that you're discovering your true self. What's important is to acknowledge the kind of person you are, and then paint a self-portrait of the way you want to become.

To become extremely happy, you have to delve into your heart and purify it. It's natural that there will be things that you don't want to see. Nonetheless, make sure that you don't let this opportunity pass you by. Bring out the contents of your heart and place them before your eyes, and accept them as they are. Since you were able to pick up this book, you should be able to do this as well. That's right, you can create your own happy future.

CHAPTER 3

Love

In this chapter we will explore things
that are vital for ensuring that every day
for you is a wonderful day. You already
know in your heart what the answers are.

Complete the following sentences:

Romance is...

Love is...

Marriage is...

Criteria for the ultimate partner...

Femininity is...

Masculinity is...

If your friend asks you for advice because he or she has fallen for somebody who already has a boyfriend or a girlfriend, what would you say?

_____

_____

_____

_____

_____

_____

_____

If your friend asks you for advice because he or she as fallen for somebody who already has a husband or wife, what would you say?

_____

_____

_____

_____

_____

_____

_____

What do you call your loved one (girlfriend or boyfriend; spouse)?

_____

_____

How would you describe your loved one in an advertisement?

_____

_____

_____

_____

_____

What animal would you compare your loved one to?

_____

What color do you associate with your loved one?

_____

What smell or fragrance do you associate with your loved one?

_____

What are some words or phrases that your loved one often uses?

_____

_____

Three of your love one's strong points:

Three of your loved one's weak points:

● If you were able to change just one of your loved one's characteristics:

✱ Which one would you change?

✱ How would you change it?

● Name a person you broke up with:

- -

✱ Why did you break up with that person?

- -

- -

- -

- -

● Name a person who broke up with you:

- -

✱ Why did that person break up with you?

- -

- -

- -

- -

Describe the most painful case of heartbreak you've experienced:

_____

_____

_____

✱ Recalling that time, write a letter to cheer yourself up:

_____

_____

_____

_____

_____

_____

✱ Freely describe the feelings you'd like to convey to the other

person involved in the situation:

_____

_____

_____

_____

_____

✸ Three things that you've learned from that broken heart:

- -

- -

- -

- -

- -

- -

✸ If you were able to become happy by praying for that other

person's happiness, how would you do this?

- -

- -

- -

- -

- -

- -

- -

- -

- -

● Have you ever betrayed your loved one?

☐ Yes ☐ No

✳ How?

_____

_____

_____

_____

✳ Does your loved one know?

☐ Yes ☐ No

● Your loved one says that something you said or did hurt them.

✳ Words or actions that come to mind?

_____

_____

_____

✳ Things you want to convey to your loved one about this:

_____

_____

_____

List several influences you think your loved one has had on you:

_____

_____

_____

_____

_____

_____

List several influences that you are grateful to your loved one for:

_____

_____

_____

_____

_____

_____

_____

● Suppose your loved one has only one month to live:

   ✽ How would you try to interact with him or her?

   _____

   _____

   _____

   _____

   ✽ How would you spend this time?

   _____

   _____

   _____

   _____

   ✽ What do you think your partner would want from you?

   _____

   _____

   _____

   _____

● Suppose you have only one month to live:

✱ How would you try to interact with your loved one?

_____

_____

_____

_____

✱ How would you spend this time with your loved one?

_____

_____

_____

_____

✱ What would you like from your loved one?

_____

_____

_____

_____

Close your eyes, take a deep breath and say "feel". Suppose that love, in a shapeless form, has entered you from a certain part of your body. Which part do you feel that would be? Give as many responses as you like:

When do you feel loved by your loved one?

Suppose you've lost your voice. How would you convey your affection to your loved one? Imagine various situations and write down specific answers:

● Imagine that you've created the ideal relationship for yourself and your loved one:

   ✱ What kind of relationship is this?

_____
_____
_____
_____
_____

   ✱ What kind of facial expression do you have?

_____
_____
_____
_____
_____
_____

To those who finished
CHAPTER

3

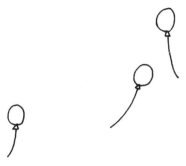

When love is going well, it's the ultimate bliss! But love isn't all roses. No matter how good love is, there will be times when you worry, and times when you feel pain.

Perhaps there are lessons to be learned that you couldn't learn in any relationship other than the one that you have with that person. Lessons learned through worry and painful struggle definitely make us grow to be human beings who can love. When a relationship with a person you don't even like becomes painful, it's relatively easy to break it off. But if you love the other person, it's a completely different story. If, however, you realize that the trauma of being in pain but not being able to let go is teaching you about love, then the way you worry may change.

Among the crucial parts of this chapter were the questions about the times you experienced a broken heart in the past. While answering the "love-scarred past" questions that I posed, were you able to get a real handle on your emotions?

Writing a letter to yourself and about the feelings that you want to convey to your partner must have made you think once more

about the past, and probably put you through various feelings.

Some people may have ended up shedding tears. But that's all right—because they were healing tears. Tears purify the heart. They are tears that show us that purification is necessary in order to lead a more pleasant life. Say to yourself, "That's all right; it's just that built-up things flowed out, and now I feel relieved."

On the other hand, if you noticed that intense feelings like anger or hatred, or the feeling of not being able to forgive, had been locked up inside of you, accept these, in a similar way as I described before. Emotions are naturally bound to exist. So realize that, if you hold a grudge forever, you will be the one who is miserable.

In fact, consider that previously locked up feelings have been freed to a certain extent. That makes this a very meaningful epiphany. Breathe deeply, gently stroke your chest over your heart, and say, "Thanks for everything up to now" and "I accept the natural emotions inside of me."

Filling in answers like this while experiencing various feelings is actually part of what counseling is about. Think of it as a "shedding of the skin" necessary to help you heal and grow a bit more.

Another crucial part of this chapter is when you were pressed into answering, "If you only had a little more time with the person you love, how would you spend it?" and "If you lost the ability to use words, how would you express your love?" The ultimate questions (circumstances) sometimes bring up the ultimate messages.

So as to not forget the answers you discovered as "things that were always removed from reality," I suggest that you put them into practice in your daily-life relationships.

If you forget to display affection, you won't be able to grow into a person who can love.

Never forget that chances abound in our daily lives to give out love and to grow.

Relationships

Taking a look at the people in your circle
— your friends and family — will help you
get a clear picture of what you look like.

● Name a person you have been friends with for the longest time:

_____

✷ How long have you been friends? _____

Friend you can talk to about anything:

_____

Friend who makes you laugh a lot:

_____

Friend you want by your side when you're heartbroken:

_____

Friend you'd want to go traveling with:

_____

Which friend would you choose to live with for six months on a

desert island?

_____

Which friend would you choose to start up a company with?

_____

List three things you think are necessary for a good friendship:

Conversational topic that you often bring up:

Conversational topic that other people often bring up:

Conversational topics that you really want to be involved in:

_____

_____

_____

_____

_____

_____

_____

_____

Conversational topics where you mostly just listen:

_____

_____

_____

_____

_____

_____

_____

_____

● Something you don't want to show anybody:

    ✱ How would you react if somebody were to see that thing?

● Something that you don't want anybody to know:

✱ How would you react if somebody were to know that thing?

Person you often have a clash of opinions with:

- -

Person you somehow feel uncomfortable around:

- -

● Person whose relationship with you is "a little off" somehow:

- -

✱ Reasons you have this relationship:

- -

- -

- -

✱ Things you want to convey to that person (without forgetting to respect that person's position and feelings):

- -

- -

- -

- -

● Person who is not very likely to rejoice at your happiness:

- -

✱ Reasons you think this:

- -

- -

- -

✱ Things you want to convey to that person (without forgetting to respect that person's position and feelings):

- -

- -

- -

✱ Person you feel positive around:

- -

✱ Person you feel negative around:

- -

✱ Difference between these two people:

- -

- -

What kind of person do you think people consider you to be?

_____

_____

_____

_____

_____

Person who most rejoiced at your being born:

_____

Person you want by your side when you die:

_____

● Person you respect:

_____

✳ Your relationship with that person:

_____

✳ Things you respect about that person:

_____

_____

_____

People in your circle that you associate with the following words:

Love:
_____

Anger:
_____

Haste:
_____

Happiness:
_____

Effort:
_____

Adventure:
_____

Competition:
_____

Justice:
_____

Jealousy:
_____

Fear:
_____

Sadness:
_____

Loneliness:
_____

Endurance:
_____

Freedom:
_____

Sincerity:
_____

Suppose a major disaster strikes the whole country and you can only contact ten people. Which ten would you choose?

(Count your mother and father as one person each.)

What you call your father:

_ _

Where your father is from:

_ _

A color you associate with your father:

_ _

A smell or fragrance you associate with you father:

_ _

How you'd describe your father in an advertisement:

_ _

_ _

_ _

Words or phrases that your father often says:

_ _

_ _

_ _

Similarities between you and your father:

Three of your father's strong points:

Three of your father's weak points:

What you call your mother:

_____

Where your mother is from:

_____

A color you associate with your mother:

_____

A smell or fragrance you associate with your mother:

_____

How you'd describe your mother in an advertisement:

_____

_____

_____

Words or phrases that your mother often says:

_____

_____

_____

chapter 4

Similarities between you and your mother:

- -

- -

- -

- -

Three of your mother's strong points:

- -

- -

- -

Three of your mother's weak points:

- -

- -

- -

● Expectations you have of your family:

_____

_____

_____

_____

   ✱ Would your life change if your family didn't fulfill your expectations?

     ☐ Yes ☐ No

● Matters you want to resolve regarding your relationship

with your family:

_____

_____

_____

   ✱ Ways of resolution that you can think of:

_____

_____

_____

● Something that was done by your parents, or father only, or mother only, that you can't forgive:

✳ What would make you forgive them?

Something that you'd apologize about to your parents, or father only, or mother only:

Suppose that your father has only one more day to live. Write a letter that expresses your heartfelt appreciation for his role in your life:

_____

_____

_____

_____

_____

_____

_____

_____

_____

_____

_____

_____

_____

_____

_____

Suppose that your mother has only one more day to live. Write a letter that expresses your heartfelt appreciation for her role in your life:

_____

_____

_____

_____

_____

_____

_____

_____

_____

_____

_____

_____

_____

_____

● Suppose "the here and now" is a drama with you in the leading role. Who would play the supporting roles? What would the theme song be?

✱ Leading actress/actor: (You)

_____

✱ Leading actor/actress:

_____

✱ Supporting actress:

_____

✱ Supporting actor:

_____

✱ Villian(s):

_____

✱ Supporting cast members:

_____

_____

✱ Theme song:

_____

● Suppose you were to make a wish or pray for somebody other than yourself:

   ✱ Who would you pray for?

_____

_____

_____

   ✱ What would you pray for them?

_____

_____

_____

_____

_____

_____

_____

_____

_____

To those who finished
CHAPTER
4

Now that you've answered the questions on relationships, what kind of discoveries did you make?

If you had an epiphany—like "I've worked out who is really important to me" or "I've discovered that I'm doing things a little unnaturally somewhere"—then you should be really happy. It would be excellent if, based on the answers that you gave, you're now able to see what you're like, you've decided to try to be a certain way, and your goals have become clear in your mind.

Do you want to try to be more self-assertive? Then in your conversations you should start immediately to try to say the things you'd normally not say. If you want to create a little distance between you and a person you have trouble getting along with, then that chance will definitely come. And when it does, please make the choice that you would normally never make (but don't forget to show consideration for others' feelings).

Your answers are cries from your heart. So don't fail to heed those cries; make a change! This way your relationships with people will be transformed.

What's important is how you felt when you were answering. (This is something that is applicable to all the chapters.)

As I've repeatedly said up to now, knowing our true feelings is very important for leading more free and happy lives. If you felt something—for example, a sense of guilt—while answering, it's actually very valuable that you were able to notice that. This is because many people complain of something being pent-up, even though they don't know which emotion is involved. Depending on the person, it may be a sense of guilt, or a feeling of irritation. When you experience emotions that you can do nothing about, as long as you notice the sensation in yourself, such emotions are certain to result in your growth.

Both the person that you like and the person that you dislike are actually parts of yourself. The good things that you perceive about the liked person are in fact your own strong points, and the unpleasant things about the disliked person are your own weak points. Thus, in disliking a certain part of that person, you are actually reproaching yourself!

I'm sure the "thank you," "sorry," and "forgiveness" parts of the questions concerning parent-child relationships allowed you

to view your feelings up until now, as well as issues you need to deal with from here on. But there's no need to feel down if you weren't able to answer those parts well. Why? Because learning where you currently stand in terms of this relationship is a major achievement in itself. If you answer the questions again awhile later, you'll probably discover that you've advanced from your present point.

If you develop the ability to learn something from any kind of relationship, you'll worry less about relationships with people. That's because you'll realize that, instead of trying to change the other person, it's easier to change yourself—and the transition is smoother. Building good relationships while growing at the same time: that's like killing two birds with one stone, don't you think?

CHAPTER **5**

Money

What does money mean to you? In this chapter, take a good, hard look at your take on those "greenback dollars."

Focusing on the positive side of money, complete the following:

Money is...

_____

_____

_____

Focusing on the negative side of money, complete the following:

Money is...

_____

_____

_____

Complete the following:

It's better to have money, but...

_____

_____

_____

● Wish List 1

 ✱ Things I want right away:

_____

_____

_____

_____

_____

_____

_____

 ✱ Things I want within a year from now:

_____

_____

_____

_____

_____

_____

_____

● Wish List 2

   ✷ Things I want within ten years from now:

_____

_____

_____

_____

_____

_____

_____

   ✷ Things I want before I die:

_____

_____

_____

_____

_____

_____

_____

● Calculate your monthly earnings and expenditures, as well as what you wish your expenditure could be:

✱ Income _____.

✱ Expenditures: Expenditure Goals

Food: _____ ➔ _____

Rent: _____ ➔ _____

Tuition: _____ ➔ _____

Clothing: _____ ➔ _____

Utilities: _____ ➔ _____

Socializing: _____ ➔ _____

Leisure: _____ ➔ _____

Medical: _____ ➔ _____

Beauty: _____ ➔ _____

Other: _____ ➔ _____

Total: _____ ➔ _____

● Estimate the amount of money that has been spent on you from the moment you were born until now:

Food:

Rent:

Tuition:

Clothing:

Utilities:

Socializing:

Leisure:

Medical:

Beauty:

Other:

Total:

✱ Looking at the total amount, how do you feel?

The richest person you know personally:

- -

Three impressions you have about rich people:

- -

- -

- -

In your view, how much income classifies somebody as rich?

- -

Your current annual income, including part-time pay and pocket money:

- -

Your current amount of savings:

- -

If you were to put a monetary value on yourself, how much would it be?

- -

If your friend asked you to lend him money, what amount would you give without hesitating?

- -

How low does the amount of money in your wallet have to go for you to become worried?

- -

● Is there anybody you've lent money to but who hasn't yet paid you back?

☐ Yes ☐ No

✱ Who?

- -

✱ How much?

- -

Things money can't buy:

_____

_____

_____

_____

_____

_____

_____

_____

_____

_____

_____

_____

_____

_____

_____

● Suppose you lent a friend $50 and he only returned $40. It seems that it's just an honest mistake. Would you:

☐ Say that there isn't enough?   ☐ Just let it go?

☐ Other:

✳ Reasons

● Suppose you're about to buy something for $50 but you're only charged $40. The salesperson seems to have missed the mistake. Would you:

☐ Say that he's mistaken?   ☐ Say nothing?

☐ Other:

✳ Reasons:

- Suppose that you could scream, "I want money!" and get $10,000. Where would you scream that?

- * Reasons for choosing that place:

- * Suppose you had to use up that money in five minutes, what—excluding the option of saving it—would you spend it on?

● For some reason, you want money. Say you can receive the amount
   of money you want if you're able to cleverly persuade God:

   ✱ What amount of money would you ask for?

   _____

   ✱ How would you start your persuasion attempt?

   _____

   _____

   _____

Suppose you were able to obtain wealth or financial success. How do you think you would change in terms of the following attributes?

Stinginess: ☐ UP ↑ ☐ DOWN ↓ ☐ SAME →

    ✳ Reasons:

Generosity: ☐ UP ↑ ☐ DOWN ↓ ☐ SAME →

    ✳ Reasons:

How jealous you become: ☐ UP ↑ ☐ DOWN ↓ ☐ SAME →

    ✳ Reasons:

Positive attitude: ☐ UP ↑ ☐ DOWN ↓ ☐ SAME →

    ✳ Reasons:

Immaturity: ☐ UP↑ ☐ DOWN↓ ☐ SAME →

   ✴ Reasons:

How much you deliberate on things: ☐ UP↑ ☐ DOWN↓ ☐ SAME →

   ✴ Reasons:

Competitiveness: ☐ UP↑ ☐ DOWN↓ ☐ SAME →

   ✴ Reasons:

Curiosity: ☐ UP↑ ☐ DOWN↓ ☐ SAME →

   ✴ Reasons:

How much you take on challenges: ☐ UP↑ ☐ DOWN↓ ☐ SAME →

   ✴ Reasons:

- Suppose there's such a thing as compatibility between a person and money. Do you think you are compatible with money?

☐ Yes ☐ No

✱ Reasons:

- On what occasions do you think you've suffered a loss, money-wise? Give as many responses as you like:

✱ In what way could you interpret this so that you don't think you've suffered a loss money-wise?

Close your eyes, breathe deeply, and just "feel." Suppose you had to relax a specific part of your body in order to become rich. Which body part do you think that would be? Give as many responses as you like:

God says, "I'll make you rich if you protect a certain something for the rest of your life." What do you think that "certain something" might be?

_____

_____

_____

_____

_____

_____

_____

_____

_____

_____

To those who finished

CHAPTER

5

Even if you don't want to be a slave to money, in this society you do need money to live. When you go out into the world, you may be evaluated at work by criteria such as your sales figures. There may be times when, if you don't have money, you'll be forced to give up what you want to do.

My experience in psychotherapeutic counseling has taught me that rich people tend to have a positive impression of money, whereas people who are always struggling with money have a negative impression of it. Many people had the latter impression driven into them by their parents when they were children. Sometimes people are told things like "money is a dirty thing" and "rich people are greedy," and at other times people are told off for the way they use money.

We all have our weak points from which we unconsciously try to distance ourselves. The same can be said about money. As long as you think that obtaining money is a shameful or greedy thing, you won't get it. But even people who feel that way can't completely deny the necessity of money, or the inner desire for it. If that's the case with you, you probably need to figure out your misperception about money, correct this, and create a mental position in which you are ready to welcome lots of it.

Were you able to honestly specify the things that you want? Are you even afraid to want things? Become a person who can feel free to desire what he or she wants. Tackle and answer questions like "What do you want?" and "How much do you want?" head-on. You may think that's impossible, but at this point you're not being asked whether it's possible. Do some practice exercises on what you want, making sure that your own negative impression doesn't get in the way.

If you were able to list what you want but had a negative impression of money, try to create a positive image based on keywords like "cash" and "abundance." Establish a perception of money that considers specific positive aspects, like the fact that it allows you to take holidays abroad and helps reduce worry about security.

And how about the huge sum of money you calculated in response to the question of how much money has been spent on you from birth until now? That may have shocked you or sent a chill down your spine.

This is an exercise in facing up to the things that are essential for humans to live. Look reality square in the face. I've counseled a person who was in debt. This person said "I'm too scared to even look at my bank balance, so I don't even know much debt I have." Averting your eyes from reality like that won't solve the problem. Write down your money-related problems clearly and organize the actions you need to carry out in order to solve them. The person I just mentioned solved his problem by facing up to reality.

The fact that we're here is reality. It's a given that we live and breathe. This is not a daydream, but reality. It is also a fact that money exists in reality. If you've realized that you've been avoiding reality, then you need to face it squarely. Once you do this your relationship with reality will improve.

Money is an amazing source of energy. It can definitely create a positive cycle — but this all depends on your state of mind.

Vision

You only live once. There are many things you can do so that you do not live in regret.

Complete the following sentences:

Life is excellent in terms of...

\- -

\- -

\- -

Life is the pits in terms of...

\- -

\- -

\- -

The original meaning of life is...

\- -

\- -

\- -

You are summoned to heaven. What kind of life would

you like to lead there?

If you were to become a person who knows no fear, what challenges would you take on? Give three examples:

● Suppose you're sentenced to live for only one more year. What kind of life would you lead?

✱ What if it were only five more years?

✱ Ten years?

Your dreams:

✻ Things you are currently doing in order to achieve them:

✱ Things you would like to do from now on to achieve them:

Complete the following series of sentences:

The happiest kind of life is...

_____

_____

_____

But now...

_____

_____

_____

Despite this, I will definitely achieve the happiest kind of life. For this goal I have to do the following five things:

Imagine that you've become the happiest you can be. Picture a circle, with yourself on the inside and the environment on the outside. What are you like? How do you feel? What kind of situation are you in? Feel free to create your own picture.

you

To those who finished
CHAPTER

Some people out there are worried because they don't have fixed dreams or goals—but I take this to be a good sign.

Why? Because worrying that you don't know what you want to be shows that you want to find your dreams and goals and to move one step closer to them. How many people do you know that have succeeded in achieving the dreams they had from their childhood? Few and far between are the people who, at an early stage, discover their own style of living and move forward from there in a straight line.

Start off by painting a picture of the kind of person that you somehow don't like, and also picture the kind of person that you want to become. When you start to enjoy yourself with that vague picture, you will naturally see what your true values are.

Once we achieve a good balance between other people's values and demands and our own true values and demands, we can achieve true happiness as individuals. There have probably been times in your own life that you have felt a gap—large or small— between other people's values and your own true values. What's important here is that you definitely cannot be happy just by living solely according to your true values. Of course, the same can be said about trying to live only according to other people's values.

If you only assert your own values, you'll become isolated and will probably experience loneliness. Conversely, even if you can meet others' demands, you won't feel as though you're living—which is not something you can call happiness.

This is when a balance of both factors becomes necessary. But balance here is not just simply 50:50. The ideal degree of balance depends on the individual. For you it may be 90:10 or 70:30. Either way, as long as you don't know what your true values are, a good balance will probably be hard to find. That's why it's extremely important that you clarify what your true values are.

What you want to become and how you want to be may appear to be two different things. Still, it can be said that they were originally the same thing. It's usually the case that when somebody has realized their dream, they've succeeded on not just a physical level, but also on a human level. The converse is also true: the closer you are to becoming your ideal person, the closer you are to achieving your ideal physical state. Thus, make sure that you visualize an overlap of these two factors as being the "ultimate state" and "ideal you." The answers that come forth at that point should be the messages you need to hear toward becoming your ideal person. This is why it's said that the real answers are within yourself.

One way to live is to choose a lifestyle based on things that you can probably do and things that are demanded of you. But you can also discover what kind of life you want to live by comparing the endless possibilities and your gut demands against your current reality, as a basis for determining the road you want to walk down.

Happiness is achieved through a feeling of fulfillment and satisfaction inside yourself. Be confident, find your own happiness, and go forward!

Postscript

There's something I want to say to you for answering all the questions: "Well done!" And "Congratulations!"

Generally in my counseling sessions, in order to extract true answers from a person, I pose questions from various angles. You need to take a good, hard look at yourself to find the answers. I know that this is not a simple thing to do. A round of applause for all your hard work!

In the process of answering the questions, you had to experience a variety of emotions. It couldn't have been easy for you: nobody really wants to feel negative emotions, such as anxiety or guilt, if they can avoid them. But going through this process one chapter after another, you succeeded in completing this entire book. This must have made you feel better and given you a great deal of power. You deserve to be congratulated on your growth.

The fact that you finished the whole book is sure to become a much stronger source of power for you than you imagine—all the more so if, having done so, you were forced to think, and feel tired as a result. The bonus is that the energy you expended will come back to you.

There are times in my counseling sessions when I use worksheets containing various questions. The person I'm counseling has to fill in the answers himself. Knowing how effective the worksheets are, I'd wanted to somehow compile them into a book. But I'd heard that "fill-in-the-blanks" books have requirements that make production and bookbinding rather difficult. Thus, for the last several years I'd set this idea aside.

Then one day I received a proposal from an editor that perfectly matched what I'd been visualizing for many years:

A "fill-in-the-blanks book" that frees the mind. It relaxes you. It allows you to get one step closer to your dreams and ideals. When you've finished it, you'll be able to see your true self.

But the production process posed two obstacles. One was that, in contrast to individual in-person sessions, I couldn't ask questions based on my understanding of each individual's personality, background and issues.

The other was that trying to achieve a "counseling effect" usually results in a serious book with questions that are difficult to answer.

That's why, on numerous occasions, I had all the staff at my publisher's office be guinea pigs to help me out. I'd like to take this opportunity to offer them my thanks. This book is a direct result of all their hard work.

I will be most happy if this book helps people who want to live more freely and happily and create their own life.

From here on, please continue to believe in yourself and endeavor to achieve your ultimate happiness.

All the answers, always, are within you!

Happiness is always around you.